Diana

The Caring Princess

Diana

The Caring Princess

In Her Own Words

Compiled by
Margaret Holder

Hodder & Stoughton
LONDON   SYDNEY   AUCKLAND

Frontispiece: The Princess with Prince Harry

Compilation copyright © Margaret Holder 1997

First published in Great Britain 1997

The right of Margaret Holder to be identified as the
Compiler of the Work has been asserted by her in accordance with the
Copyright, Designs and Patents Act 1988.

1 3 5 7 9 10 8 6 4 2

British Library Cataloguing in Publication Data
A record for this book is available from the British Library

ISBN 0 340 71422 0

Typeset in ITC Galliard and originated by
Strathmore Publishing Services, London N7

Printed and bound in Great Britain by
Mackays PLC, Chatham, Kent

Hodder and Stoughton Ltd
A Division of Hodder Headline PLC
338 Euston Road
London NW1 3BH

Contents

On Love   7

Introduction   11

Diana's Approach to Life   19

The Family and Relationships   25

Children   33

Women's Health   47

Disabled People   55

Elderly People   65

International Concerns   71

Leprosy   87

Drug Addiction   91

AIDS Patients   99

The Ill and Dying   107

Epilogue   121

Illustration Sources   125

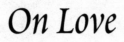

On Love

If I speak in the tongues of men and of angels, but have not love, I am only a resounding gong or a clanging cymbal. If I have the gift of prophecy and can fathom all mysteries and all knowledge, and if I have a faith than can move mountains, but have not love, I am nothing. If I give all I possess to the poor and surrender my body to the flames, but have not love, I gain nothing.

Love is patient, love is kind. It does not envy, it does not boast, it is not proud. It is not rude, it is not self-seeking, it is not easily angered, it keeps no record of wrongs. Love does not delight in evil but rejoices with the truth. It always protects, always trusts, always hopes, always perseveres.

Love never fails. But where there are prophecies, they will cease; where there are tongues, they will be stilled; where there is knowledge, it will pass away. For we know in part and we prophesy in part, but when perfection comes, the imperfect disappears. When I was a child, I talked like a child, I thought like a child, I reasoned like a child. When I became a man, I put childish ways behind me. Now we see but a poor reflection as in a mirror; then we shall see face to face. Now I know in part; then I shall know fully, even as I am fully known.

And now these three remain: faith, hope and love. But the greatest of these is love.

1 Corinthians, Chapter 13,
which was read at the funeral
of Diana, Princess of Wales

Introduction

Diana, Princess of Wales, was a humanitarian and compassionate woman. This compassion and this feeling for fellow human beings shone like a beacon in her charity work. It was this, together with a charismatic character, an attractiveness to the media and a professionalism about her work, that combined to make Diana, Princess of Wales, one of the strongest supporters any charity could wish to have working for them. Her involvement with the British Red Cross from 1983 was invaluable.

Having seen, at first hand, the love and care that Diana, Princess of Wales, gave to elderly people, refugees, children, cancer victims, people who were HIV-positive or who had AIDS, and landmine victims, there is no doubt that she was a woman who could combine her personal qualities with the power and interest of the media in order to make things happen.

This was no more true than with her recent involvement in the Red Cross Anti-personnel Landmines Campaign. When I met with the Princess in December 1996 to discuss her possible involvement in the Landmines Campaign, she wanted to know the facts. She wanted to know whether or not her involvement would make a difference; she wanted to know whether what she had to offer would assist the worldwide campaign for a global ban on the use and production of anti-personnel landmines; and also she wanted to know whether or not her contribution would help those who were victims. She especially wanted to help women and children, who were suffering the terrible consequences of picking up or stepping on an anti-personnel landmine. There was no doubt in my mind, and indeed no doubt in the mind of Diana, Princess of Wales, that her intervention would help.

There followed a frenetic few weeks as we planned her involvement in a major event to raise funds for the victims of landmines and, perhaps more importantly, a visit to Angola in January 1997 to see for herself the devastation caused by these savage and indiscriminately laid weapons.

The effect of the Angola trip on the Landmines Campaign far exceeded our wildest dreams. There can be few people in the world today who do not now know of the overwhelming damage caused by the indiscriminate use of anti-personnel landmines. As a result of the Princess's work, a great many more people believe that these barbaric weapons of war must be banned.

On her arrival in Angola, the Princess said,

I am absolutely delighted to be in Angola and to be given this opportunity to play a part in helping the Red Cross in its worldwide campaign to ban anti-personnel landmines.

Civilians, including women and children, are among the innocent victims of these indiscriminate weapons and are often doing nothing more than working or playing in the fields when they sustain their injuries. There is one landmine for every sixteen children in the world.

I hope that we can all work together during the next few days and beyond to focus world attention on this issue.

During the flight from London to Luanda, the capital of Angola, I sat next to her to give her briefings on the visit ahead. She worked on her speech, even though it was prepared beforehand, and I was impressed by her professional approach.

Later in the flight, the Princess asked me for my advice on the clothes she should wear during the visit. I was initially puzzled that the woman who led the world of fashion would ask me such a question. She explained that she wanted to be sure to give the clear impression to everyone who saw her that she

was going to Angola on a working visit. I noted later
that it was thought by some members of the press to
be very unusual for the Princess to dress informally
and I realised the importance of her decision to wear
a simple white blouse, beige trousers and flat shoes.
The Princess was using her knowledge of the media
to help strengthen people's understanding of her role
for the Red Cross.

The Princess's concern for people who were
suffering from horrific injuries caused by landmines
came through on many occasions during this visit to
Angola. We saw her encouragement to 13-year-old
Sandra, who had lost her left leg when she stepped
on a mine while looking after her younger brother as
her mother searched for wood. We saw the Princess
sympathising with a father who had lost both his
legs when a mine exploded and who was unable to
work and provide for his family of seven children.
We saw her gently comforting 7-year-old Helena
who had suffered severe intestinal injuries caused by
a mine explosion when she was fetching water. I
could see that the Princess was moved and upset by
what she saw, and angry about their unnecessary suffering. In each case, Diana, Princess of Wales, left
them with hope. She will always be remembered for
sharing this gift of giving hope to others.

I know that this caring attitude was a normal and regular part of the Princess's life.

When returning with her on an overnight flight to London from Washington, following a major Red Cross fund-raising event, she arranged for one of her staff to drive me home in the early hours of the morning. I hadn't asked her to do that and I hadn't mentioned that I needed transport home. In no small way, I experienced for myself her natural ability to care and to think of others. When I accompanied the Princess on her visit to Zimbabwe in July 1993 to view the Red Cross drought relief operations and refugee camps, she changed her schedule to enable her to visit AIDS patients privately.

I remember well the impact the Princess made when, in November 1992, she opened Red Cross House, Irvine complex in Inverness. This is a unique project of the British Red Cross which provides facilities and services to help people with disabilities to learn to live an independent life in the community. During her visit, the Princess motivated staff and residents. She was very friendly and quickly put people at their ease as she chatted with those she met. At the end of the visit I was pleasantly surprised when she even offered me a lift back to London on the Queen's flight!

Her words contained in this book illustrate the many occasions she used her special gifts and the unforgettable impact she made on so many people's lives. The legacy to the world of Diana, Princess of Wales, is a living one. As a humanitarian ambassador she effectively shared her compassion and commitment to help people who were suffering, and in doing so motivated others to take similar positive action to change the world for the better.

Mike Whitlam
Director General
British Red Cross Society

Diana's Approach to Life

There are two basic agents when defining us as human beings – one, a sharpness of mind. Two is kindness of the heart – hearing and sharing the grief of others.

– Receiving
Humanitarian of the Year Award, 1995.

I pay great attention to people and I always remember them. Every visit, every meeting is special. Nothing brings me more happiness than trying to help the most vulnerable people in society. It is a goal and essential part of my life, a kind of destiny. Whoever is in distress can call on me. I will come running, wherever they are.

– Last interview given in June 1997 to
Le Monde *and published by the Paris-based paper*
a few days before she died there.

I feel close to people whoever they might be. We are all the same to begin with, on the same wavelength. That is why I disturb certain people.

Because I am closer to people down there than to people higher up they won't forgive me for that. Because I really have close relations with the most humble people.

– Interview with Le Monde, *published shortly before she died.*

I want the boys to experience what most people already know – that they are growing up in a multi-racial society in which not everyone is rich, has four holidays a year, speaks standard English and has a Range Rover.

– Diana's hopes for her sons, expressed to friends, 1994.

It's prayer, Tony, prayer. It is most important.

> *– Private words to the Revd Tony Lloyd,*
> *Executive Director of the Leprosy Mission,*
> *who had commented,*
> *"I don't know how you stay sane." 1993.*

I find that fascinating and enticing.

> *– Private words about the afterlife*
> *to the Revd Tony Lloyd, Executive Director*
> *of the Leprosy Mission, 1993. Diana had*
> *long discussions about religion and*
> *spirituality with him. She was interested in*
> *conventional religions as much as*
> *astrology and psychic guidance.*
> *Lloyd believes she was simply seeking*
> *after the truth.*

The Family and Relationships

With Princes William and Harry
at Niagara Falls, Canada

My father always taught me to treat everyone as an equal. I have always done and I am sure that William and Harry are the same.

– Interview with Le Monde *newspaper, 1997.*

As a mother of two small boys, I think we may have to find a secure way of helping our children – to nurture and prepare them to face life as confident and stable adults.

– Televised address as President of Barnardo's, 1988.

I want to bring them up with security. I hug my children to death and get into bed with them at night. I always feed them love and affection; it's so important.

– Words about her sons,
William and Harry, around 1992,
when they were ten and eight.

Harry has some kind of bug and isn't very well. I did not have a very good night's sleep because he was climbing into my bed. I feel sad and a bit guilty leaving him to turn up for jobs like this one when one of my own children isn't well.

> – *A maternal confession to a playgroup leader in Hillingdon, London, 1987. Another helper said, "It was just like talking to any other mother."*

My first priority will continue to be our children, William and Harry, who deserve as much love and care and attention as I am able to give, as well as an appreciation of the tradition into which they were born.

> – *Speech to 'Headway' charity, when she temporarily retired from public life, 1993.*

If we can do a proper job of giving our children the affection which nature demands I believe it will help enormously. Hugging has no harmful side effects. If we all play our part in making our children feel valued, the result will be tremendous. There are potential 'huggers' in every household.

> – *Seminar at launch of European Drug Prevention Week, 1992.*

During my visits to Barnardo's work I see a very strong commitment to family life. Of course, what constitutes a family today is much broader than in the past. There are single-parent families, permanent foster families and increasingly complicated families resulting from separation, divorce and remarriage. But love, commitment and sharing together are essential ingredients of family life, whatever its form, and it is our task to do all we can to enable children to benefit from it.

> – *Foreword to* Barnardo's Review, *1990. Diana's family life was complicated; her parents had divorced and remarried; she had seven step-siblings. It gave her insight into the problems of children she tried to help.*

The award is really intended as a tribute to the thousands of families whose daily lives are constructive, loving and unselfish. These are the families who give the best to each other and to society while quietly coping with a daunting array of pressures.

– Presenting Family of the Year Award, 1990.

I know from my own visits to their offices around the country that the experts of Relate have daily contact with the distress which underlies the statistics ... Most couples discover and draw on new resources of love and strength. But for many their own resources are not enough.

– Speech, praising work of Relate at the Family of the Year Luncheon, 1990.

Christmas is a time which can be lonely, can be sad, but it can also bring joy, laughter, light, and a time of great blessings to so many.

> – *Foreword to* Once Upon a Christmas, *compiled by Esther Rantzen for Childline, 1996.*

If an Englishman's home is his castle – then what happens when he has no home? And what if an Englishman is young – perhaps mid-teens, early twenties – what greater risks will confront him?

These are the questions which Centrepoint boldly faces each day of the year. And it's doing a tremendous job in helping us understand the real extent and nature of Britain's homeless population.

It is customary at this time of the year to focus attention on those less fortunate than ourselves. But homelessness is an experience which isn't confined to the festive season. It is not a problem that miraculously appears on the first day of Christmas and then disappears on the twelfth. It is a daily problem for many in our towns and cities and Centrepoint is at work each day of every year.

Neither are the homeless made up of 20- and 30-year-olds who have had their chance at life and some failed miserably. The age of homeless youngsters is coming down. Children as young as eleven called at Centrepoint this year.

> *– From a stirring speech delivered at Centrepoint's Annual Conference, 1996. Homeless young people, often escaping physical and emotional cruelty, were part of Diana's 'constituency of the rejected', as her brother movingly called those on the extremities of life whom she tried to help. She sometimes took her sons to meet the down-and-outs, to see for themselves a side of life that many prefer to forget.*

A lot of people watch TV and play so many video games these days they don't really talk to one another... People should be spending time together instead of everybody being glued to the box.

> *– Comments during a conversation with the mother of a child presenting her with flowers at Great Ormond Street Hospital for Sick Children, 1993.*

Children

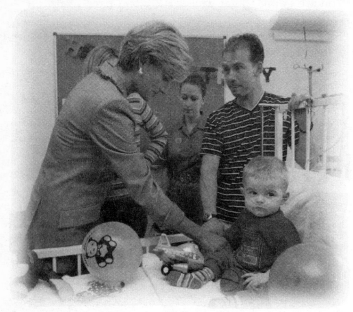

At the Paediatric Intensive Care Unit at St Mary's Hospital, London

You are going to get well again – you have youth on your side.

> *– To a child seriously ill with pneumonia in 1996.*
> *The 11-year-old girl was coming out of a coma and*
> *was expected to remain at least eight weeks in St*
> *Mary's Hospital, Paddington. The girl's mother found*
> *that Diana was visiting the hospital and approached*
> *her in a corridor. Diana went straight to the child*
> *who recovered so well that she went home three days*
> *later. "It was a miracle," said the mother.*

Have you met any other girls who have been through the same experience? Do you think it might help? I think you might find other young people would make you feel you did exactly the right thing.

> *– Wise and sensitive words to a girl whose father*
> *had been imprisoned for appalling cruelty after she*
> *contacted Childline. The girl felt guilty for the*
> *consequences of her actions. Diana managed*
> *to convey her total approval and suggested*
> *positive ways the girl could find to help herself.*
> *Childline's London opening, 1988.*

Children need every chance available to help them along the difficult path to adulthood. A good education, a safe place to live and play, and someone who will listen are all essential ingredients of a decent start in life. Yet many miss out on these seemingly ordinary requirements. Barnardo's continues to work to help make their path a little smoother.

— From the foreword of Barnardo's Review, 1996. Diana wrote a foreword each year as President. She was passionately interested in the charity and all aspects of its work for twelve years. Sadly, it was one of the hundred or so she gave up after losing the title 'Her Royal Highness' upon her divorce in 1996.

I'm terribly distressed. What happens to these children? How can we help these children through this? How can we stop it happening?

— Words to Esther Rantzen, founder of Childline, after visiting the charity's headquarters and listening to calls from desperate children, 1988.

In Tokyo at the National Children's Hospital

I fully realise that for many young people family life is not always a happy experience. They may have been thrown out of their own homes or circumstances may have forced them to leave. Some are homeless, some at risk of drug addiction or prostitution.

– Annual General Meeting of Barnardo's, 1988. Diana had been President for four years and had made many visits to centres. She was very supportive of foster care provided by the charity which seeks to keep families united wherever possible, and was keen to help young people on the edge of society through Barnardo's and other organisations.

I take my teddy to bed every night and he travels with me everywhere I go.

– Diana revealed her secret to a 5-year-old girl recovering from a serious infection at Poole General Hospital in 1988. It was typical of her instant rapport with children.

In Brazil

Of course you can come for a drive in my car.

– Reply to a 3-year-old AIDS victim, known as 'Little Lady', at an AIDS children's home in New York, USA, in 1990. Diana personally carried the girl to her official Rolls Royce (see picture opposite).

As parents, teachers, family and friends, we have an obligation to care for our children. To encourage and guide, nourish and nurture, and to listen with love to their needs in ways which clearly show our children that we value them.

They in turn will then learn how to value themselves.

– Speech at a conference about eating disorders, 1993.

Opposite: Carrying 'Little Lady' to the car in New York

Of course you can give me a hug.

– To a child in a crowd in Liverpool who rushed up to her, in April 1982. This breach of royal protocol was one of the earliest instances of Diana's caring side.

Follow me around. You can be my lady-in-waiting.

– Words to a 5-year-old girl, one of 150 people evacuated from their homes during the floods in North Wales in 1990.

Opposite: Princess Diana at the Birmingham Institute for Conductive Education in 1995

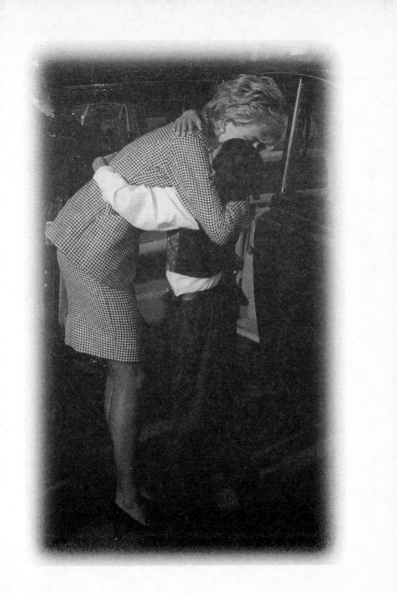

I'm a great lover of children and the fact that a little person can have a second opportunity from my country – I'm very proud to be involved. You gather information much more from a visual contact rather than reading books.

So when I stand up and speak about the various subjects, whatever it is, it's more beneficial if I've actually seen it for myself.

– Words to a reporter after watching Sir Magdi Yacoub perform heart surgery on a 7-year-old boy, flown in from the Cameroon for this life-saving operation, 1996.

I would ask everyone who is buying something for a child this Christmas, however small, to ensure that it is totally safe.

– Speech at the annual meeting of the Child Accident Prevention Trust, in 1988. She spoke as the mother of two small "inquisitive" boys, adding that she knew how easy it was for accidents to happen.

Like millions of others, I was deeply shocked after hearing of the tragedy that your school has suffered.

I know that my words are inadequate but I wanted you to know that everyone who heard the news will silently share your grief. I hope you will find comfort and strength by hearing their prayers and mine.

– Taken from a letter to the headteacher of Dunblane Primary School, Scotland, after sixteen young children and their teacher were shot and killed. Diana wrote the letter on the day of the tragedy in 1996.

Women's Health

If we, as a society, continue to disable women by encouraging them to believe they should only do things that are thought to benefit their family, even if these women are 'damaged' in the process, if they feel they never have the right to do anything that is just for themselves, if they feel they must sacrifice everything for their loved ones, even at the cost of their own health, their inner strength and their own self-worth, they will only live in the shadow of others and their mental health will suffer.

– *Women and Mental Health Seminar, 1990.*

Isn't it normal not to be able to cope all of the time? Isn't it normal for women as well as men to feel frustrated with life? Isn't it normal to feel angry and want to change a situation that is hurting?

– *Women and Mental Health Seminar, 1993.*

For decades, tranquillisers, sleeping pills and anti-depressants have been given to a generation of women – three times as many as to men. These 'mother's little helpers' have left a legacy of millions of women doomed to a life of dependence from which there is very little escape.

– *Women and Mental Health Seminar, 1993.*

They need another hostel.

– *Subtle hint to housing chiefs in Luton, Bedfordshire, after she had spent an hour in a Women's Aid hostel for battered wives and their children, in 1986.*

From the beginning of time the human race has had a deep and powerful relationship with food... Eating food has always been about survival, but also about caring and nurturing the ones we love.

However, with the added pressures of modern life, it has now become an expression of how we feel about ourselves and how we want others to feel about us.

Eating disorders, whether it be anorexia or bulimia, show how individuals can turn the nourishment of the body into a painful attack on themselves and they have at their core a far deeper problem that mere vanity.

– Diana spelled out her beliefs about eating disorders in a passionately delivered address in 1993. She spoke of the low self-esteem and distress which accompanies these illnesses. She had suffered from bulimia for much of her adult life and had begun the process of conquering her illness. Typically, she wanted other people to understand these disorders and she encouraged many sufferers to find treatment.

Despite information about AIDS being available for nearly ten years, these women still face harassment, job loss, isolation, even physical aggression, if their family secret gets out...

Relentless demands continue to be placed on her when her own health and strength are falling away. As well as the physical drain, a mother with HIV carries the grief and guilt that she probably won't see her children through to independence.

– Speech at the Second Conference on HIV in Children and Mothers at the Heriot-Watt University, Edinburgh, in 1993. This issue focused some of the themes close to Diana in her last years: care of children, family problems, women's health, and AIDS.

In June 1996 with Aileen Getty, the 36-year-old second child of J. Paul Getty, Jr., one of the longest-surviving women with AIDS

Disabled People

I don't know how I would cope if I had a child who was handicapped or mentally handicapped in some way. So I'm going out there, meeting these children, and I'm learning all the time and trying to understand, trying desperately to understand how they cope.

– Interviewed in 1985, Diana talked about her interest in handicapped children, particularly as President of Barnardo's.

I'll bet you have some fun chasing the soap around the bath.

– Diana's special touch was evident here. She met a nervous, one-armed, elderly man at a Help the Aged home, in 1986. He laughed and joked with the Princess, later describing her as "gorgeous".

Touch my face. I don't mind at all.

> *– To a blind man, aged twenty-two. He had asked if he could touch her to find out if she was as beautiful as people said. Diana knelt in front of him and placed his hand on her face, in 1995. Blind people often sensed Diana's magnetic personality, although deprived of her beauty and glamour which entranced so many sighted people (see picture opposite).*

I hope you will always be able to let others share in your own strength.

> *– From a letter to a cerebral palsy victim, a woman of twenty-seven who had met Diana through the Chicken Shed, a theatre company which welcomes young people of all abilities. Diana also wrote a foreword to her book,* Paula's Story, *1993.*

Thank you.

> *– Not spoken, but in sign language by a touch on the chin, to a 5-year-old deaf and partially blind girl who could only manage the word 'hello' in sign language. At an awards ceremony for brave children trying to overcome handicaps, in 1988.*

Don't worry, I can't smell it because I had a Chinese meal last night.

> *– A quick-witted response to a 32-year-old paraplegic patient at Lodgemoor Hospital, Sheffield, in 1994. He had apologised for the unpleasant aroma of liniment on his body during his keep-fit routine.*

Opposite: Diana using sign language

How incredible it is that people with these disabilities can carry on as normal and get on with their lives.

> *– Praise for severely disabled athletes at the Paralympic Games, Stoke Mandeville, in 1984, to members of the Federation of Small Businesses who had organised the events.*

Elderly People

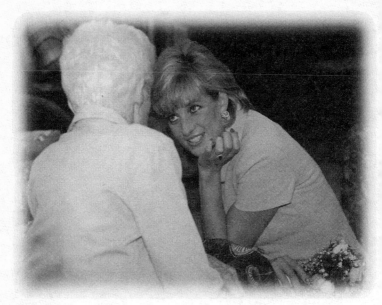

*At the British American Benevolent
Society in Argentina*

Growing old is, sadly, not always fun. There are elderly people in this country who fear for their financial and physical security. Many are concerned about their health, many are frail and worried about living an independent life.

– From an early public speech, when her warmth and understanding were beginning to shine through the routine palace rhetoric of prepared statements. She was trying to inject personal concern into areas with which she sympathised. Help the Aged's Silver Jubilee Reception, 1986.

It is tragic that elderly people cannot afford high electric and fuel bills.

– To a disabled pensioner at a Help the Aged day centre in 1986. When the woman told her that she went to bed to escape the cold, Diana replied, "I suppose that's the best place to keep warm." Later, the pensioner said, "Diana really does care for the elderly. She is an inspiration to us."

At a refugee camp in Hungary

I wouldn't dream of asking your age. I asked where
you came from.

> *– A quick-witted reply to a hard-of-hearing
> man who told her he was ninety-one, at a
> Help the Aged home in 1985. Staff
> often commented on her ability to
> communicate easily with the elderly.*

Try to keep your spirits up.

> *– Words to an 82-year-old woman
> dying of cancer who told Diana
> she wanted to see the daffodils
> bloom again, in 1986.*

International Concerns

In a landmines cleared area in Angola

I'm a humanitarian, not a political figure... All I'm trying to do is help. I am trying to highlight a problem that is going on all around the world.

– A remarkably controlled response to criticism from certain politicians in Britain who had ridiculed her landmines mission and referred to her as a 'loose cannon'. By then she had seen the appalling devastation on life and land. The plight of maimed and often homeless victims in Angola and other war-torn regions of the world became her last crusade.

A lot of information started to arrive on my desk and the pictures were so horrific that I felt if I could be part of a team to raise the profile around the world, it would help.

– Explanation of how she came to be involved in the anti-landmines campaign, January 1997. After her death, a hundred nations signed a pact banning them.

You read the statistics, but actually going into the centres and seeing them struggling to gain a life again after they have had something ripped off by something on the ground – it is shocking.

I have seen some horrifying things over the years, but I have learned to cope with it because each person is an individual, each person needs a bit of love. You don't think about yourself.

– Words to members of the press accompanying her on the Angolan minefields mission, 1997.

I looked into their eyes and saw it all.

– Diana's reply to the head of the Red Cross Federation in 1997 in Luanda, Angola, who had told her, "If you really want to see the effects of mines, look around you."

In Tuzla, Bosnia

I have seen lots of poverty before but I have never seen such devastation.

– Sarajevo, Bosnia, 1997. Diana's last mission for her anti-landmines crusade (see picture opposite).

The waste of life, limb and land which anti-personnel mines are causing among some of the poorest people on earth is a waste of which our world is too unaware, for the mine is a stealthy killer long after the conflict is ended.

– Speech, Washington, 1997.

Having seen for myself the devastation that anti-personnel mines cause, I am committed to supporting in whatever way I can the international campaign to outlaw these dreadful weapons.

– Speech, Washington, 1997.

*In Sarajevo: Diana's last mission for her
anti-landmines crusade*

In hospital at Humbo

Just looking at her and wondering what was going on inside her head and heart was very disturbing, yet she was just one of the statistics. It was very touching.

> *– Diana told the Red Cross that the most*
> *poignant memory of her January 1997*
> *mission to the Angolan minefields was the sight of*
> *a 7-year-old girl whose intestines had been blown out.*
> *Kept alive by a saline drip, the child, who was still*
> *conscious, did not know who Diana was.*
> *"Is she an angel?" she asked*
> *(see photograph opposite).*

It is very sad that you are facing a lot of problems ... changing people's attitudes is a slow process.

> *– Words of commiseration to the president of an associ-*
> *ation for Asian women whose community centre had*
> *been vandalised, in 1991. Diana showed great skill*
> *and understanding in communicating with minority*
> *groups – she made people feel valued.*

I was enormously impressed by the genuineness of your approach to the survivors and their families to sustain their morale and to help them maintain their self-esteem.

Their tragic stories are a desperately sad reflection of man's inhumanity to man. The victims I have met and their senselessly inflicted injuries have stiffened my resolve to ensure that their needs for care and support are not overlooked in the search for an agreement to outlaw landmines.

> – *Part of one of Diana's last letters, written 12 August 1997, to Jerry White, co-founder of the Landmines Survivors Network.*

It's too early to say when I will go but if the activities carry on much longer, I might well do so. I'm very concerned about the morale of the troops and I'm keen to go.

> – *Words to members of the public during a walkabout in Portsmouth, October 1990, when British troops were already in the Gulf and Britain was on a war-footing with Iraq. Prince Charles was sent there instead. Diana later comforted the waiting wives.*

In Bosnia with Elvira Tadil, comforting her in her grief. Sometimes no words were necessary.

You are not forgotten, especially at Christmas-time. There is nothing that I could say which will fill that gap in your lives, and to say that I, along with so many others at home, understand and sympathise with you at this time sounds very inadequate and rather too easy. But it is the least I can do, and I do feel for you, with all my heart.

– Speech to wives of British soldiers serving in the Gulf War, 1991 (see photograph opposite).

I shall never complain again.

– Words to members of the press after coming out of a peasant's hut in a remote area of Nepal in 1993. The single room was cold, dark, and thick with smoke; it was home to a whole family.

With wives of soldiers in the Gulf

Diana's words to Mother Teresa, who met her on several occasions, remain private. It is known that Diana wanted to spend some time helping her order, the Missionaries of Charity, in India. When Diana died, Mother Teresa said, "She helped me to help the poor. That's the most beautiful thing."

> *— Mother Teresa died aged eighty-seven on 5 September, the eve of Diana's funeral. She was writing a letter of condolence as she died.*

Opposite: With Mother Teresa in New York

Leprosy

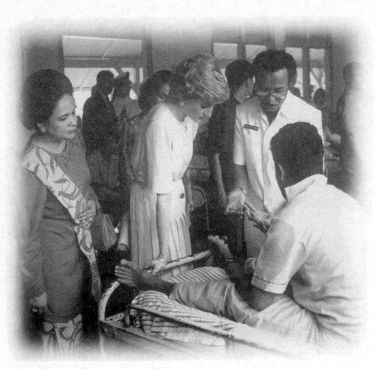

In a leprosy hospital in Jakarta, Indonesia

I play that at home. Who's winning?

> *– A chat, via an interpreter, with two*
> *12-year-old boys afflicted with leprosy*
> *in a lepers' hospital, Jakarta, Indonesia, in 1989.*
> *They were playing chess; Diana picked up*
> *a piece that had rolled under a bed. She went on*
> *to touch disfigured limbs and faces, even touching*
> *blood-soaked bandages to dispel the centuries-old*
> *superstition that leprosy is caught*
> *by casual contact.*

I didn't feel sorry for her, it's a joy. I was happy for her – it's wonderful what has happened to her.

> – *At a leprosy hospital in 1989 Diana found a woman with hardly any fingers making a dress with a treadle sewing-machine. A nurse told Diana, "She came here a leper and is leaving as a Christian seamstress." The Princess went behind a screen to cry, then explained her emotions to the accompanying members of the Leprosy Mission.*

We must always leave them with hope ... that's the most important thing.

> – *At Tongagara refugee camp on the Harare/Mozambique border in 1993, Diana found a very sick woman lying on the ground. She crouched down and held the gnarled hands of the woman, who was badly afflicted with leprosy. Diana said these words on that occasion, and on others, to members of the Leprosy Mission.*

Drug Addiction

Drug abuse is becoming more and more widespread. Addiction knows no class barriers. I'm extremely concerned as any mother would be.

– In 1986, Diana was the first of many celebrities to sign a huge 'Say No to Drugs' pledge organised by Westminster City Council.

Very often it is in the home that the climate for addiction is created and, equally often, it is in the home that its worst consequences are felt.

A stable domestic background, where the simple duties of family life are shared and understood, can do much to strengthen those tempted to find a refuge in drink or drugs.

– From a powerful address to a symposium arranged by Turning Point, a charity which helps addiction sufferers, 1989.

Addiction can strike any who suffer distress in their personal or professional lives.

Alcohol and drugs do not respect age, sex, class or occupation and the line between recreational use and creeping addiction is perilously thin.

– From her address to a symposium on addiction as Patron of Turning Point, 1989.

These should be shown on television so everyone could see the damage smoking does.

– Remarks to doctors at the British Lung Foundation, Brompton Hospital, London, after being shown slides of diseased lungs in 1986.

If the immediate family breaks up, the problems created can still be resolved. But only if the children have been brought up from the very start with the feeling that they were wanted, loved and valued. Then they are better able to cope with such crises and better able to build around them their own affection groups.

They'll make friends more easily, find fulfilment in team sports and be better able to build a collective spirit in the workplace or in their community. These are all platforms of mutual affection which help us to survive.

Children who have received the affection they deserve will usually continue to recognise how good it feels, how right it feels, and will create that feeling around them. We've all seen the families of the skilled survivors. Their strength comes from within, and was put there by means of learning how to give and receive affection, without restraint or embarrassment, from their earliest days.

– Speech at the European Drug Prevention Week Media Seminar, 17 November 1992. Often considered one of Diana's finest speeches, this was made at a time of great personal turmoil. She and Prince Charles were almost at the point of separation – the official announcement was made on 9 December. As she spoke she must have had her own children in mind, perhaps voicing fears and hopes as well as stating her beliefs about parental and family roles.

Learning to like yourself is the hardest thing … everyone has to come to terms with their problems.

– Words to reformed drug addicts, November 1993.
A few days later, clearly under enormous strain,
Diana temporarily retired from public life.

I'm delighted. Smoking is an unhealthy habit. I welcome any step forward in making people more aware of the importance of good health.

– Words to a Bath hotel manager, who had set aside
a third of rooms for non-smokers, in 1990. A
dedicated non-smoker, Diana even had
NO SMOKING signs at her
Kensington Palace home.

With Julie Town at Turning Point Clinic in Wakefield, UK. Julie was a drug addict who was inspired by Diana to kick the habit.

Don't be harsh on yourself.

> *– Sympathetic words to a former drug addict*
> *and anorexia sufferer at a Turning Point*
> *clinic in 1992. Diana privately admitted she*
> *had her own problems with food. This*
> *uninhibited style, combined with a gentle*
> *touch on the arm or hand, left a lasting*
> *feeling of sincerity – enough in many*
> *cases to ensure that people with eating or*
> *addiction problems resolved to*
> *improve their lives.*

I missed my boys at Christmas and the New Year.
I spent Christmas alone in Kensington Palace.

> *– Part of an astonishing chat with a*
> *self-confessed drug courier at a Centrepoint*
> *hostel, in January 1995. Even more amazing*
> *is that William and Harry, then thirteen and*
> *eleven, were with their mother. Diana was*
> *determined to show them the less attractive side*
> *of life, a world away from their cosseted life*
> *behind palace walls. And the drug peddler?*
> *He vowed there and then, "I want nothing*
> *more to do with drugs."*

AIDS Patients

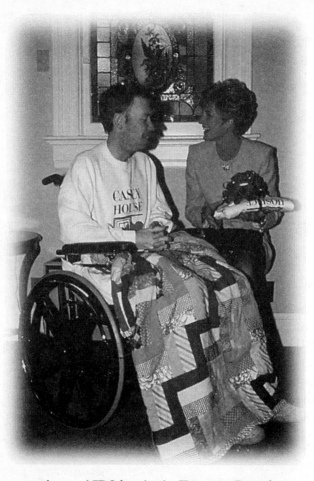

At an AIDS hospice in Toronto, Canada

No one else will help these people and I feel I must do something.

> *– Said to friends in a spirit of compassion for AIDS victims as much as in a spirit of defiance against more traditional courtiers who advised her to keep away from an area they thought unsuitable for a young princess, in 1991.*

> *Arguably, Diana did more than any other celebrity in bringing attention to the sufferings of HIV-positive people and AIDS patients. AIDS and leprosy, the twin symbols of fear and ignorance – one modern, one ancient – became personal crusades.*

I've taken William and Harry to people dying of AIDS – albeit I told them it was cancer. I've taken the children to all sorts of areas where I'm not sure anyone of that age in this family has been before. And they have a knowledge. They may never use it, but the seed is there and I hope it will grow, because knowledge is power.

> – Panorama *interview, 1995*

Don't get up. You can't get away, anyway. You seem very attached! You are very brave. I'm very bad with needles. It makes me feel dizzy just looking at you.

– Words to an AIDS patient having a blood transfusion while Diana shook hands with him, in 1988.

For me, one of the particularly sad things about my visits has been to find out how much stigma people with AIDS and HIV still suffer and how much they feel they have to deal with prejudice as well as their physical problems.

– From one of several speeches about HIV and AIDS. Diana treated the issue with enormous sympathy and compassion. She was horrified to learn that about 22 million men, women and children are affected worldwide. Similarly, she worked to eradicate the stigma of leprosy, which has 32 million direct or indirect victims.

Opposite: Holding an HIV-positive baby in a hospital for abandoned children in Sao Paulo

It meant so much to me that you were there last night. I am thinking of you.

— A private note to a young mother dying of AIDS, contracted through a blood transfusion. She had already lost one child to AIDS and was Diana's special guest at a Christmas reception at Kensington Palace in 1994. The Princess had previously visited the woman and her sick child in hospital.

You should see me in the mornings.

— To a 19-year-old man with AIDS. He had said, "You're more gorgeous than in the papers." Diana's repartee ensured an easy conversation with AIDS sufferers. She often asked her minders to stay outside so she could have a private chat with victims.

I think this belongs to you.

> *– Diana took a stone out of her shoe and handed it
> to an official of the Terrence Higgins Trust at an
> AIDS project in 1989. Sufferers and carers had
> been warned about protocol and security. Diana
> broke the ice immediately with her sense of fun.*

Your tie and shirt don't match.

> *– Typical of Diana's unorthodox way of deflecting
> tension in very sick people, these words were said to a
> 46-year-old man suffering from AIDS at the
> Mortimer Market Centre, London, on 1 December
> 1994 – World AIDS Day. He replied, "You should see
> my socks." After the visit he said, "The encouragement
> she gives to people is outstanding."*

The Ill and Dying

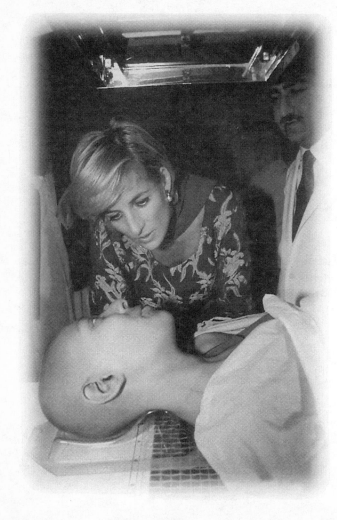

Machines always seem to go wrong when I'm around.

> *– Diana made light of an embarrassing moment when a brain scanner broke down at the National Hospital for Nervous Diseases. She comforted the patient waiting for a scan with a lighthearted, "Poor you." As ever, her sureness of touch defused an awkward situation.*

I respected very much the honesty I found on that level. In hospices, for instance, when people are dying, they're much more open and vulnerable and much more real than other people.

> – Panorama *interview, 1995.*

Opposite: With a cancer patient in Pakistan

After I had been round the first ward, I remember it so vividly. I was struck by the calmness of the patients in their beds in confronting their illness. They were so brave about it and made me feel so humble.

> *– Recalling her first hospice visit during a television interview, 1985.*

I want to hug you.

> *– Diana made private phone calls to the parents of two boys killed in the IRA bombing in Warrington, in 1993. This was said to the mother of one of the victims. Diana had wanted to visit the scene and pay her respects, but was prevented by palace advisers.*

It is a word of just six letters but has the power to strike panic, fear and anxiety into the hearts of us all ... From where I sit, looking in from the outside, I sense that the fight has begun.

– Speech at the National Museum Building, Washington, in aid of the Nina Hyde Centre for Breast Cancer Research, in 1996.

It must be very difficult for the whole family, but you have very good support. You support each other.

– Words to the heartbroken family of a cancer patient at Northwestern Memorial Hospital, Chicago, in 1996. Diana put her arm around the man's crying wife as she spoke.

I wouldn't have minded if I'd been a train driver. I've always enjoyed getting up early in the mornings. I do my chores before going out on official engagements.

– Words spoken gently to a 64-year-old retired train driver, dying of cancer in St Joseph's Hospice, Hackney, London, in 1985. Thought to have hours to live, the man survived a further six days. His widow said, "I'll always believe that was a special gift from the Princess." She gave consent for Diana's conversation to be included in a television documentary.

It has been said that for evil to triumph good men must do nothing. Tonight, we give heartfelt thanks that a good man, Dr Victor Chang, did a great deal and that we can all be thankful as we look forward to the future.

– Speech at the Victor Chang Cardiac Research Institute Dinner, Sydney, Australia, in 1996. Chang, Australia's leading heart transplant surgeon, had been murdered in 1991.

Diana at St Joseph's Hospice

I just thought I'd pop in for a cuppa.

> *– On the doorstep of a car-crash victim, Dean Woodward, whom Diana had met in 1991 when Charles was being treated for a broken arm after a polo accident the previous year. Diana had stroked Dean's forehead as he came out of a coma and had befriended his family. She called at his tiny council-owned house to check on his recovery and sat with his two young children on her knees. Diana wrote frequently to the family.*

I am thinking of you constantly and you're in my prayers throughout the day. Keep strong.

> *– From a personal letter to Dean's mother, Ivy Woodward. Diana sent this letter when she heard his mother was ill, in 1991.*

With Dean Woodward

There are few subjects more likely to raise anxiety and fear than cancer. It seems to strike out of nowhere, destroying lives at will, leaving devastation in its wake.

While few of us may be able to pioneer a new form of surgery or test a new drug, we can support those who do. We can raise money for research and work in other ways to ensure that the fight against this disease continues to press ahead.

– Speech at a symposium on breast cancer at Northwestern University, Chicago, in 1996. Diana attended as President of the Royal Marsden Hospital, which was one of the major beneficiaries of her dress auction held by Christies, in New York, two months before she died.

I'll bring you a bottle when I'm passing this way.

– Words to a cancer patient at a Sue Ryder Home, in 1984. The man complained to Diana that he couldn't get his favourite beer. She sent him a case of twenty-four bottles.

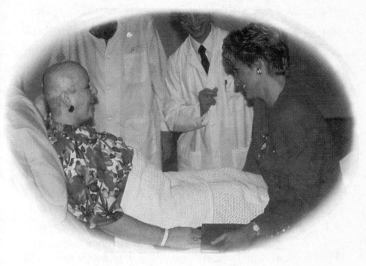

*Visiting Northeastern Ontario
Regional Cancer Centre, Canada*

These people – cancer patients or people with other illnesses – they come out of the operating theatre and come round alone. I try to be there for them. Some will live and some won't – but they all need to be loved while they're here.

– Explanation about her hospital visits, in 1995.
She regularly visited two London hospitals and
stayed with seriously ill patients. While she gave so
much to help others, she also gained a sense of
self-worth in an often turbulent life.

You look much better than when I last saw you. I'll see you again at the weekend. God bless you.

– On visiting in hospital the tramp she had
helped to rescue by raising the alarm when he
fell into Regent's Park canal. She gave him a
get-well card and some money. He said,
"The lady's a miracle to me."

You only have to spend a short time at the Royal Marsden Hospital to feel its special atmosphere of care, confidence and cheerful efficiency.

The methods of treatment pioneered by this hospital and the caring skills of its staff have enabled thousands of people to face cancer with hope and have laid to rest the myths and stigma that have for so long surrounded the disease and its treatment.

Sadly, all the goodwill in the world cannot meet the continuing demands for better facilities, more sophisticated technology and new developments, which is why we should all bring to this hospital the support it deserves.

– Diana's foreword to an information brochure produced in 1997 by the Royal Marsden Hospital, of which she remained President after her divorce and the loss of her title.

It has been one of my greatest privileges to be present when a cardio-thoracic operation was carried out. It was an amazing and enlightening experience. But even more amazing was the effect on the patient. The return of hope on the faces of family and friends is something I will never forget.

– Speech at a fund-raising dinner held at Harrods for Sir Magdi Yacoub's Heart Science Research Centre, Harefield Hospital, in 1996. The host was Harrods' owner, Mohamed al Fayed, whose son, Dodi, would be Diana's last companion. By tragic irony, Diana underwent emergency heart surgery in Paris in the early hours of 31 August 1997. Despite the heroic efforts of doctors at the Pitié Salpêtrière Hospital, she died at 3 a.m. British Summer Time.

Epilogue

Diana in Sarajevo, a few weeks before her own death

Life is mostly froth and bubble
Two things stand like stone
Kindness in another's trouble
Courage in your own.

– Words of the Australian poet, Adam Lindsay Gordon, quoted by Diana at a fund-raising dinner at the National Museum Building, Washington, in 1996. The lines could almost be her epitaph.

Illustration Sources

ℰ ILLUSTRATION SOURCES ℘

Author and publisher are grateful to the following for permission to use the photographs:

page	
frontispiece	Tim Graham
26	Tim Graham
34	Tim Graham
37	Tim Graham
39	Tim Graham
41	Tim Graham
43	Kent Gavin, Mirror Syndication International
53	Tim Graham
56	Tim Graham
58	Martin Keene, PA News
60	Tim Graham
62	Tim Graham
66	Tim Graham
68	Tim Graham
72	Arthur Edwards, the *Sun*
75	Ian Jones, FSP/Gamma
77	Ian Jones, FSP/Gamma
78	Arthur Edwards, the *Sun*
81	Tim Rooke, Rex Features
83	Tim Graham
85	Charles Sykes, Rex Features

88 Tim Graham
97 Mirror Syndication International
100 Tim Graham
103 Tim Graham
108 Tim Rooke, Rex Features
113 Tim Graham
115 Raymonds Press Agency
117 Tim Graham
122 Ian Jones, FSP/Gamma